W9-BZC-212

MARY EMMERLING'S
AMERICAN COUNTRY
Flags

★

FOR MY MOTHER, FROM HER DAUGHTER

AND

FOR MY DAUGHTER, FROM HER MOTHER

Text copyright © 1991 by Mary Emmerling
Photographs copyright © 1991 by Joshua Greene

All rights reserved. No part of this book may be reproduced or transmitted in any form or by any means, electronic or mechanical, including photocopying, recording, or by any information storage and retrieval system, without permission in writing from the publisher.

Published by Clarkson Potter/Publishers, New York, New York.
Member of the Crown Publishing Group.

Random House, Inc. New York, Toronto, London, Sydney, Auckland
www.randomhouse.com

CLARKSON N. POTTER is a trademark and POTTER and colophon are registered trademarks of Random House, Inc.

Printed in the United States of America

Design by Renato Stanisic

Library of Congress Cataloging-in-Publication Data
Emmerling, Mary
Mary Emmerling's American Country Flags/photographs by Joshua Greene.
1.   Emmerling, Mary Ellisor—Themes, motives. 2. U.S.—Flags—Pictorial Works. 3. Flags in art. 4. Folk art—U.S. I. Emmerling, Mary Ellisor. II. Greene, Joshua. III. American Country Flags
NK839.E46A4   1991
929.9'2'0973—dc20   91-13325

ISBN 1-4000-4530-4

10 9 8 7 6 5 4 3 2 1

First 2001 Edition

MARY EMMERLING'S
AMERICAN COUNTRY
Flags

PHOTOGRAPHS BY JOSHUA GREENE

Clarkson Potter/Publishers
New York

For over two hundred years, even before the invention of our nation, the stars and stripes, and the colors red, white, and blue have symbolized our country's pursuit of liberty. Since the beginning, Americans have expressed their affection for this symbol of national pride by designing and making flags, by running them up flag poles, carrying them in parades, and draping them over heroes' coffins. And the flag and its elements can be found on countless wonderful examples of country furnishings, baskets, quilts, and folk art carvings. This is not just because the American people are patriotic, but also because the flag itself, like any enduring symbol, has both beauty and meaning. Its strong graphic elements attract our attention and remind us of something that is important to us all. ★ As our nation grows older, and we have more history to tell, the flag becomes even more important to us than it was in the days of the Revolutionary War. During the Civil War, the flag stood for unity when the country was painfully divided. When Americans moved West they took the flag with them and it became part of Native American culture, woven into pictorial blankets by the Navajos and worked into beaded moccasins by the Plains Indians. ★ With the first Centennial in 1876, school children waved tiny flags, and commemorative memorabilia of every conceivable kind used flags as a primary ornament. One hundred years ago, when my great-great-great grandfather Benjamin Harrison was president, the flag found its way onto pillows, banners, invitations, scarves, and dance cards—the attic at the Benjamin Harrison home in Indianapolis is still crammed with wonderful treasures. ★ I have always loved the American flag, probably because I grew up in Washington, D.C., where every government building, every national memorial site flies a flag year-round. The Washington Monument, with flags all around its base, filled me with pride every time I saw it as a child. Flags came out by the thousands when heads of state and other dignitaries visited and by the millions when the new presidents were inaugurated. In the summers we left town and went to Rehoboth Beach, Delaware, but the flag always came with us; we unfurled it and set it out as soon as we arrived—a sign that we were home. The Fourth of July marked the middle—and the high point—of summer, and came with its red, white, and blue bunting, streamers, fireworks, and more flags. But for me the flag was the motif of the whole season: Every year I had a small flag waving from the handlebars of my bike.

★ About twenty years ago my family started to spend summers in Waitsfield, Vermont, which has, in my opinion, one of the best Fourth of July parades in the country, old-fashioned but with wonderful floats and music. Vermont is one of the oldest states in the country, and has a treasure trove of flags and patriotic memorabilia. Once I discovered a few collector's items, I was hooked. I almost bought a house just to get at the flag collection in the attic. Now I collect any flag in folk art—from flea markets, antiques stores, or auction houses, and admire flags when I see them in other people's homes. In the summer I hang an enormous American flag at the beach, connecting my cottage with those of my children. We even named our dog Star and bought him a red, white, and blue collar. ★ Flags can mean celebration and fun, but they have a serious side, too. The saddest but the most moving day of my life was when my father, Julian G. Ellisor, was buried at Arlington National Cemetery. When the guardsmen folded the flag and presented it to my mother as the planes flew in formation overhead, I was profoundly touched—I still get chills when I remember that moment. ★ Until industrial mills began manufacturing flags, and the precise details of the flag were regulated, flags were homemade and varied from maker to maker, with slightly irregular stars and slightly uneven stripes. The colors would always be red, white, and blue, but the variation in dyes gave each flag an individual character. I am the first one to believe that the fifty-star flag should be respected—and I certainly wouldn't hang it upside down or leave it to face the elements all winter—but I love old flags, too, and I love the decorative use of the stars and stripes as well as the official display. It is a symbol that means so much to us; it should be seen everywhere—not just at the post office! ★ Whether you display, collect, or merely admire flags, I hope you enjoy those assembled in *American Country Flags*—a celebration of more than two hundred years of a great American symbol.

Mary Emmerling

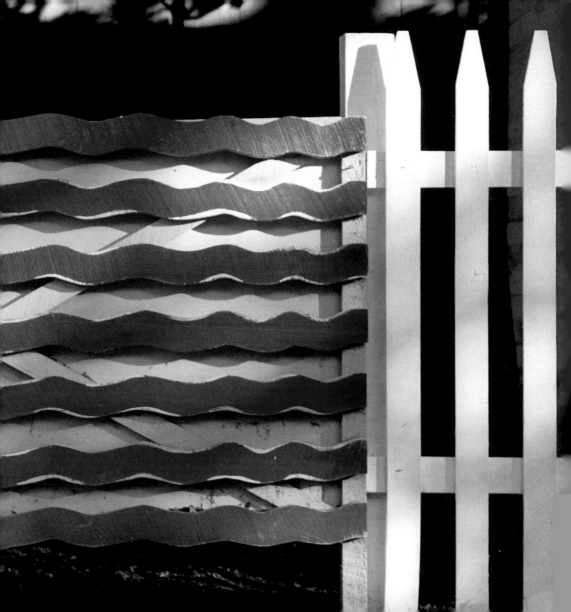

Oh, say, does that
star-spangled banner yet wave
O'er the land of the free and the
home of the brave?

Francis Scott Key

★

Flag of the brave! thy folds shall fly,
The sign of hope and triumph high.

JOSEPH RODMAN DRAKE

★

A ray of bright glory now beams from afar,
The American ensign now sparkles a star,
Which shall shortly flame wide through all the skies.

MASSACHUSETTS SPY, MAY 10, 1774

★

The love of liberty is the love of others.

WILLIAM HAZLITT

★

America is a land of wonders, in which everything is in constant motion and every change seems an improvement.

ALEXIS DE TOCQUEVILLE

★

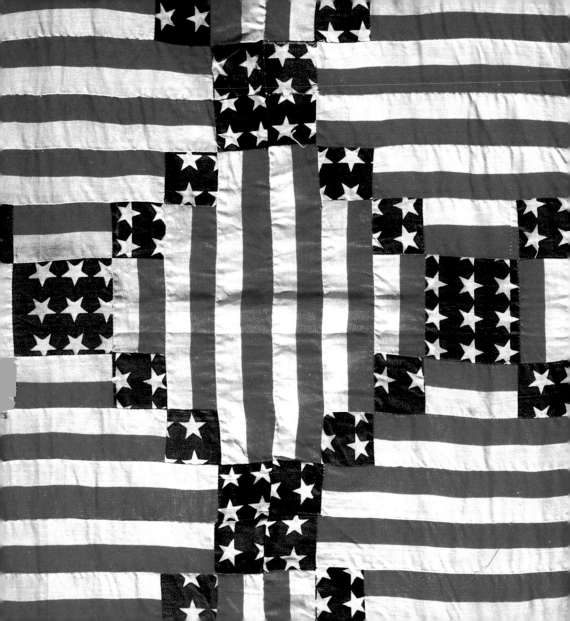

Its glorious stars in azure shine,
The radiant heraldry of heaven;
Its stripes in beauteous order twine,
The emblems of our Union given.

ANONYMOUS

★

Fling out, fling out, with cheer and shout,
To all the winds Our Country's Banner!
Be every bar, and every star,
Displayed in full and glorious manner!

ABRAHAM COLES

★

Having learned to stand by the flag,
we may also learn to stand by what the flag symbolizes;
to stand up for equal rights,
universal freedom, for justice to all,
for a true republic.

JAMES F. CLARKE

★

So it's home again, and home again,
America for me.
My heart is turning home again, and
there I long to be.

HENRY VAN DYKE

★

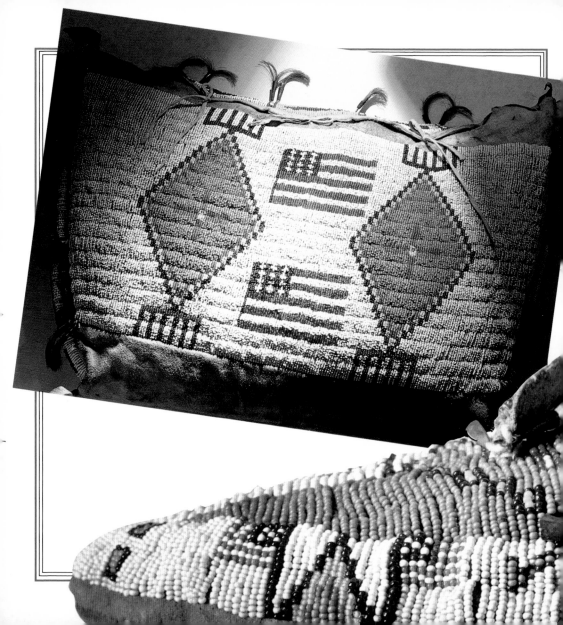

Such is the patriot's boast, where'er we roam,
His first best country is ever at home.

OLIVER GOLDSMITH

★

The United States
themselves are essentially
the greatest poem.

WALT WHITMAN

★

The union of lakes—the union of lands—
The union of States none can sever—
The union of hearts—the union of hands—
And the flag of our union for ever!

GEORGE P. MORRIS

★

White is for purity; red for valor; blue for justice.
And altogether, bunting, stripes, stars, and colors
make the flag of our country, to be
cherished by all our hearts, to be upheld by all our hands.

<small>CHARLES SUMNER</small>

★

Liberty, when it begins to take root,
is a plant of rapid growth.

GEORGE WASHINGTON

★

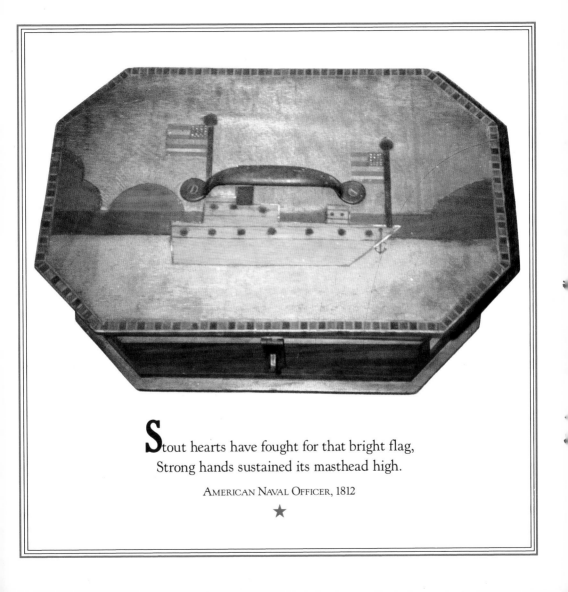

Stout hearts have fought for that bright flag,
Strong hands sustained its masthead high.

AMERICAN NAVAL OFFICER, 1812

★

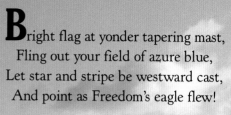

Bright flag at yonder tapering mast,
Fling out your field of azure blue,
Let star and stripe be westward cast,
And point as Freedom's eagle flew!

N. P. WILLIS

★

The fairest vision on which these eyes ever looked
was the flag of my country in a foreign land.

GEORGE FRISBIE HOAR

★

Change of Address

m May 1st 1990

the new address of

vid & Katrin Cargill

will be

9 ROWENA CRESCENT

ONDON SW11 2PT

e Number 071: 223 4499

18—CAPE HENLOPEN LIGHTHOUSE, REHOBOTH BEACH

21—Beach, Boardwalk, and Cottage Line looking North, Rehoboth Beach, Delaware

HAMPTON CLASSIC

GRAND PRIX

Arrival and Unloading of a Turtle Boat, Key West, Florida

Obeautiful for spacious skies,
For amber waves of grain,
For purple mountain majesties
Above the fruited plain!
America! America!
God shed his grace on thee
And crown thy good with brotherhood
From sea to shining sea.

KATHARINE LEE BATES

★

Its red for love, and its white for law,
And its blue for the hope that our forefathers saw,
Of a larger liberty.

Unknown

★

In a word, I want an
American character,
that the powers of Europe
may be convinced we
act for ourselves, and not for others.

GEORGE WASHINGTON

★

There is no land
like America for true
cheerfulness and lightheartedness.

WILLIAM DEAN HOWELLS

★

There is the National flag. He must be cold, indeed, who can look upon its folds rippling in the breeze without pride of country.
If in a foreign land, the flag is companionship, and country itself, with all its endearments.

Charles Sumner

★

The whole inspiration
of our life as a nation
flows out from the waving folds
of this banner.

ANONYMOUS

★

B E R N.

PEACE WE LOVE WAR IF OP-
BEST PRESSED.

TRUTH IS POWERFUL,
&
WILL PREVAIL.

America is something only if it consists of all of us;
and it can consist of all of us only as our spirits are banded
together in a common enterprise.
That common enterprise is the enterprise of
liberty and justice and right.

WOODROW WILSON

★

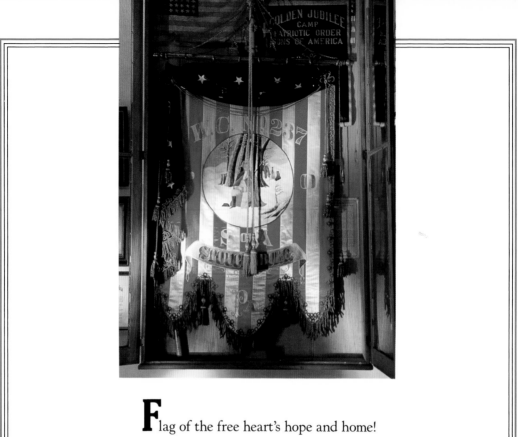

Flag of the free heart's hope and home!
By angel hands to valor given;
Thy stars have lit the welkin dome,
And all thy hues were born in heaven.

JOSEPH RODMAN DRAKE

★

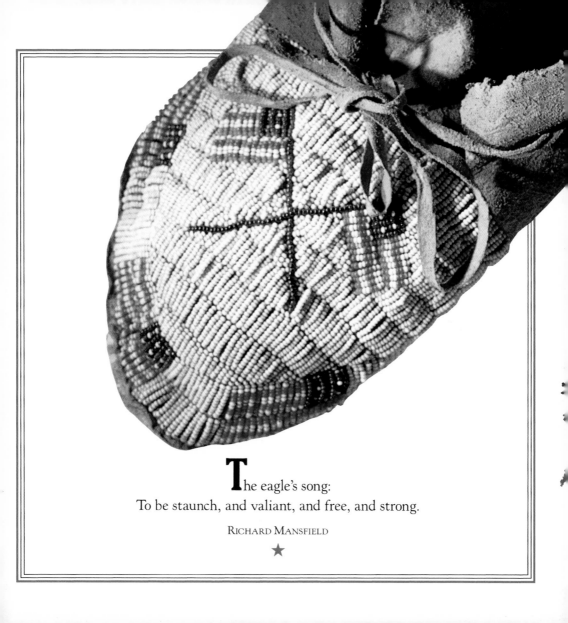

The eagle's song:
To be staunch, and valiant, and free, and strong.

RICHARD MANSFIELD

★

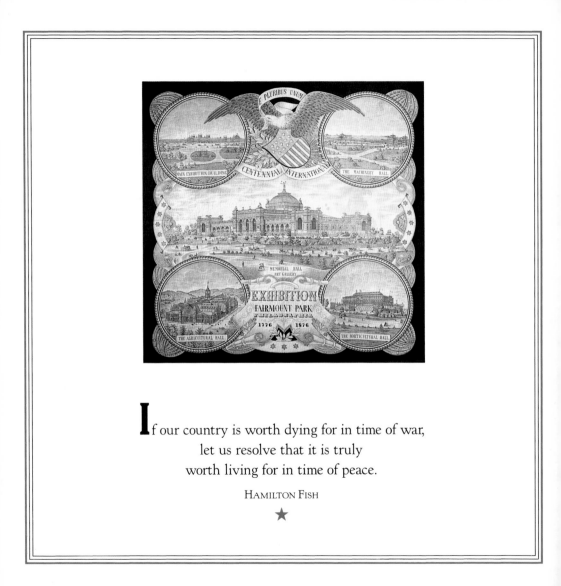

If our country is worth dying for in time of war,
let us resolve that it is truly
worth living for in time of peace.

HAMILTON FISH

★

Here may I not ask you to carry those
inscriptions that now hang on the walls into your
homes, into the schools of your city, into all of
your great institutions where children are gathered,
and teach them that the eye of the young and
the old should look upon that flag as one of
the familiar glories of every American?

BENJAMIN HARRISON

Photo Credits

Photographs by Joshua Greene: pages 5, 6, 10, 11, 12–13, 14, 15 (above), 16, 17, 19, 20, 21, 22, 23 (above), 24–25, 27, 30, 31, 32, 33, 35 (above), 36 (above), 38 (above), 39, 40, 41, 42, 43, 44, 45, 48, 50, 52 (above), 53, 56, 57, 58, 60, 61, 62–63, 64, 65 (below), 66, 67, 69, 70, 71, 72, 73, 74, 77, 78, 79, 80

Photographs by Michael Skott: pages 8–9, 18 (above), 51, 54–55

With special thanks for all the flag collectors:

Lester and Barbara Breininger, pages 27, 45, 48, 56, 57, 70, 72; Jimmie Cramer and Dean Johnson; Joe Eula, page 77; Laura Fisher Antique Qulits and Americana, pages 12, 14, 20, 30, 62, 74, 76; Pat and Rich Garthoeffner, page 59; Charlotte Grubb, page 23 (top); Lewis Keister Antiques, pages 36, 37; Jolie Kelter and Michael Malcé, Kelter Malcé Antiques; Patti Kenner, page 18; Joel and Kate Kopp, America Hurrah Antiques, pages 4, 6, 21, 28–29, 32, 33, 34, 35, 37, 46, 47, 65, 68, 69, 73, 75; Salli and Welling Lagrone, pages 26, 38; Naomi Leff, pages 58, 63, 65; Richard Martino, page 41; Lee Mindel, page 71; Bettie Mintz, Museum of American Folk Art, New York, page 46, photo courtesy America Hurrah; Ellen O'Neill, page 67; Susan Parrish Antiques, pages 14, 22, 36, 61, 64; Bonnie Rowlands Antiques, page 23 (below); John Saul's Antiques, page 49; Sandra J. Whetson, page 52 (below), 65 (above)

And with personal love and thanks to:

Lauren Shakely
Catherine Sustana
Gayle Benderoff
Carol Southern
Hilary Bass
Howard Klein
Renato Stanisic
Joan Denman
Amy Boorstein
Eliza Rand
Jonathan and
Samantha Emmerling
Juanita Jones
Michael Skott
Joshua Greene